*Front cover:*
Churn station was located high on the windswept Berkshire Downs, without road access of any sort. Despite its isolated location, it attracted a not inconsiderable amount of attention from photographers, as witness Trevor Owen's delightful view of '63xx' Mogul No 6313 heading south and about to enter the island platform on 27 February 1960, just one week from the end of through passenger workings between Didcot and Winchester. *T. B. Owen/Colour-Rail TY28*

*Back cover:*
From the vantage point of the station footbridge — Winchester and Compton were the only stations on the line provided with such a luxury — No 3212 enters Winchester's down platform on its way to Southampton, some time during the 1950s. Above the carriages the starting signal was at one time used for services heading north from the down platform, but was little used after about 1940 when the Sunday milk service was withdrawn. *S. C. Townroe/Colour-Rail*

*Right:*
The 1942/3 wartime improvements saw the route doubled as far south as Woodhay and extended loops provided at the remaining stations. In this way line capacity could be increased without the additional expense of opening out a number of cuttings that had been subject to considerable chalk falls over the years. A consequence of the extended loops was, according to the crews, considerably improved track quality where the new lines had been laid, which compared well with the hunting that was commonplace elsewhere. Seen here is another Class 4, No 76062, entering the loop at Burghclere from the north with an Eastleigh goods on 5 March 1960. *T. B. Owen/Colour-Rail/T214*

First published 2002

ISBN 0 7110 2955 5

© Ian Allan Publishing Ltd 2002

Published by Ian Allan Publishing

an imprint of Ian Allan Publishing Ltd, Hersham, Surrey KT12 4RG.
Printed by Ian Allan Printing Ltd, Hersham, Surrey KT12 4RG.

Code: 0208/B1

Ian Allan
60th
ANNIVERSARY

# On Didcot, Newbury & Southampton Lines
## Kevin Robertson

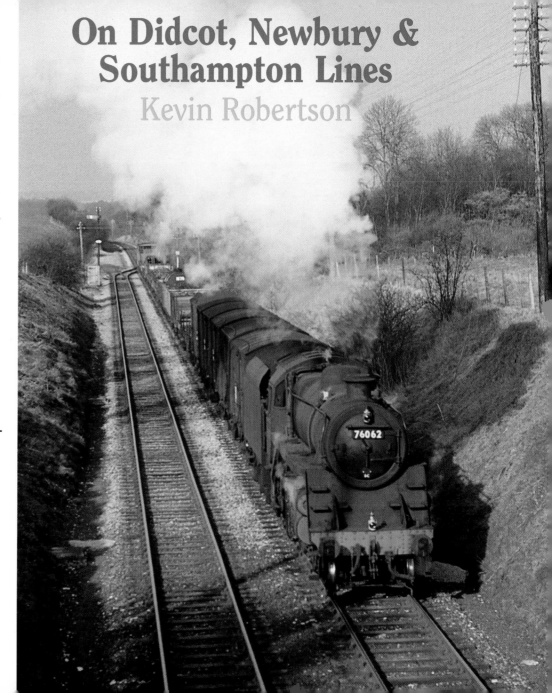

# Introduction

Forty years ago, in the summer of 1962, regular passenger services ceased to run on the last, northern, section of the former Didcot, Newbury & Southampton Railway (DN&SR). At the time there were the customary wreaths and murmured regrets voiced by those witnessing the occasion, although many of those present were seeing the line for the first time, with the regular travellers vastly outnumbered. Two years earlier in the spring of 1960 a similar fate had befallen the section south from Newbury to Winchester. The latter location was the end of the DN&S proper, although some 12 miles short of its avowed intended destination, Southampton, as indeed witnessed from the name of the original company.

At the time the little line, just over 44 miles in length, was not particularly well known, being just another cross-country route which, as far as the enthusiast was concerned, had long stood in the shadow of its neighbours, the Midland & South Western Junction Railway (M&SWJR) and the Somerset & Dorset Railway (S&DR). Unlike the other two railways, the DN&S had never possessed its own locomotives and stock, instead being operated by the Great Western Railway (GWR) from the outset, although its infrastructure of uniquely designed station buildings and houses displayed an independence that set it apart from many other routes incorporated into the GWR where a hotchpotch of architectural styles was seen.

Ironically, it is in the years since its demise — freight struggled on for a few years after the end of passenger workings but the last vestige was gone by the spring of 1966 — that the greatest interest has been generated. For whilst the line may have been unknown to many when it was running, since its closure its memory has certainly been kept alive and there is a continuing interest in its history.

That history can be directly traced back to 1873 when a company called the Didcot, Newbury & Southampton Junction Railway was formed to build a line south from Didcot, which would cross the GWR at Newbury, to a junction with the London & South Western Railway (LSWR) just north of Micheldever station. After many false starts and failed attempts at raising capital, the whole undertaking was on the verge of abandonment but was rescued by a group of influential landowners, resulting in the first section from Didcot to Newbury being opened in 1882. At Newbury there was a junction with the Berks & Hants Railway route which replaced the originally envisaged flyover.

Efforts were then made to complete the line south, with a new intention of abandoning the Micheldever connection and reaching Southampton instead. This was partly successful in that the company eventually got as far as Winchester in 1885, but there the capital ran out completely, and the railway was left with a dead-end branch from Newbury, still some 12 miles short of Southampton.

Various attempts were made to raise the necessary additional funds but all were unsuccessful and in the end the DN&S was baled out by the LSWR with a connection into its own main line, just two miles south of Winchester at what became known as Shawford Junction. One of the conditions for this financial assistance was that the DN&S would renounce all aims of an independent route to the coast, the LSWR being careful in this way to preserve its monopoly of what was extremely lucrative traffic from the expanding docks. Had it not done so, the GWR may well have decided to fund

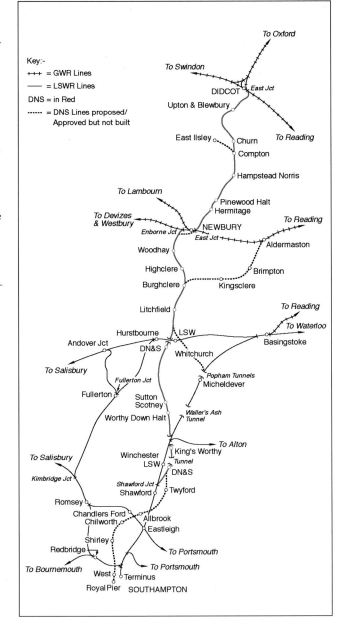

Key:-
+++ = GWR Lines
— = LSWR Lines
DNS = in Red
----- = DNS Lines proposed/ Approved but not built

the completion of the DN&S itself at some stage. However, in the end, any such ideas were never proceeded with. Similarly, the various plans discussed by the little company for expansion to Portsmouth, Bournemouth, Basingstoke, Quainton Road and Aldermaston, as well as for various short stub branch lines off its main route, all came to nothing. Had they materialised, the DN&S could well have become as renowned as perhaps the Somerset & Dorset.

Instead, the little line formed a connection between two major rivals. Built for double track but with only a single line laid, it never developed as its promoters, directors and indeed its shareholders might have wished. After all, why should either the GWR or LSWR divert traffic over the DN&S rather than keep it on their own metals?

For 50 years, then, from 1891 — the date of the completion of the extension from Winchester to Shawford Junction — the line was a rural backwater. Absorbed by the GWR from 1923, its main revenue came from agricultural traffic, whilst passenger numbers were at best limited. All this, though, would change during World War 2 in consequence of the need for improved transport links to the South Coast, in preparation for D-Day. The railway was rebuilt through much of its length, a double track provided between Didcot and Woodhay, and extended loops and new signalling installed for the remainder south to Winchester. Together with its neighbour, the M&SWJ, which was similarly although perhaps not quite so expansively modernised, the DN&S fulfilled a vital role — the very purpose that had been envisaged by the original promoters of a main north-south link.

The wartime traffic peaks, though, would disappear almost as quickly as they had arrived and the line reverted to its backwater status, although now with the added disadvantage of increased operating costs consequent upon its numerous new facilities, allied to ever-dwindling revenue. Small wonder then that the first signs of economy came as early as 1950 and continued through until passenger services were understandably withdrawn at the beginning of the 1960s. As such, its demise pre-dated the Beeching axe and to many it was a surprise that it lasted as long as it did.

Having been involved in several written works on the route, I have presented in this book a collection of colour views of the line. While some colour pictures of the line have appeared from time to time elsewhere, until now there has never been the opportunity to produce a solely colour book on what was a fascinating railway. This has become possible through the good offices of several friends and I would especially like to thank Ron White at Colour-Rail, the Townroe family and the Rev David Littlefair for permission to use their unique material. Others are credited in the captions for the individual views — if any errors have been made in this way I sincerely apologise. The end result is a reminder of earlier times, which I, like many others, took for granted as always likely to exist. Time, however, is a good teacher and many is the regret that it is no longer possible to travel by train — as I did so many times on Saturdays — between Winchester and Newbury. .

*Kevin Robertson*
June 2002

Although previously seen elsewhere, the historic importance of this view, dating from the immediate prewar period, makes its inclusion essential. The photograph was in fact taken at King's Worthy although elsewhere it has been incorrectly stated to have been Worthy Down. The train, headed by a 'Dukedog', is just leaving the station, heading north, and passing the loading dock where the end of a horse-box, or PACO, is just visible. Horse-box traffic was a regular feature on the line almost to the end, with several local stables served by the station. *Colour-Rail/GW67*

3

*Above:* Colour photographs of the DN&S line in prewar days are rare, indeed only the two reproduced within these pages are known of at the present time. We can then only imagine a time when double-framed locomotives were a daily occurrence, although a glimpse perhaps of those halcyon days can be gained from No 3256 *Guinevere* waiting in the down bay at Newbury in April 1939. The view is perhaps typical of how those of us not old enough to remember such scenes for ourselves picture the period: blue skies and apparent tranquillity. In the background the railcar waits before its journey to Lambourn, GW diesel cars having taken over most of the services on that GWR branch in 1936. They would never do the same on the DN&S. *Colour-Rail/GW16*

*Right:* As a starting point for our main journey down the DN&S line, it is appropriate to 'board the train' at Didcot, where 'T9' No 30313 is seen awaiting departure south. Eastleigh-based locomotives and crews began working some of the services over the route from 1953 after the closure of the engine shed at Winchester. Shortly after this time one Eastleigh crew having a lay-over at Didcot took their engine to shed prior to the booked return working. They were resting in the mess room when a harassed foreman came running in, shouting, '. . . move that *******  engine of yours now, it's blocking the shed and my men won't touch it . . .'! *Alan Jarvis*

*Above:* In an ideal world all views used in a book such as this would be from the same period, and every location would be featured. Sadly, reality does not allow for such luxuries and so our other view of Didcot is of the bay at the east end of the down main, from which most services to and from Newbury would be dealt with. Here '61xx' No 6145 awaits departure for Newbury on 17 February 1962 at the head of just two coaches, indicative of the limited traffic that prevailed after the section south from Newbury had been closed to passengers. The trackwork in the bay allowed for an engine release crossover and also a loading dock for horse traffic, as horse-boxes were also dealt with at Didcot. All this, though, is now more than a generation ago, and for some years the area here has been part of the car park for the present station. *Kevin Robertson collection*

*Right:* Leaving Didcot, the northern section of the DN&S was double track (after 1942) all the way to Newbury. The track layout at Didcot East Junction was such that a train from the bay platform could gain access to the route without fouling the main line — hence the trailing connection in the foreground. On this occasion, though, the train from which the view was taken, on 28 April 1959, has commenced from the main station itself. With 'T9' No 30313 at its head, it is about to pass an Eastleigh-based '76xxx' which is shortly to join the main line, probably heading north. *Alan Jarvis*

Away from the bustle of Didcot, the first station proper on the route was at Upton & Blewbury. Serving the villages of the same name, it was typical of the stations on the route, with the main station building on one side and only a wooden shelter on the opposite platform. '2251' class No 3206 was a regular performer on the line for many years and is depicted here waiting to leave southwards for Churn on 2 November 1958. *T. B. Owen/Colour-Rail R612*

Pannier tank No 4649 is pictured heading north from Churn on 27 February 1960, with the station in the background. The working is probably between Newbury and Didcot, possibly even the daily pick-up goods which ran once in each direction on weekdays. It would not, though, have called at Churn as from 1942 there had been no siding facility at the station. *T. B. Owen/Colour-Rail T25*

*Above:* Named engines were rarely seen on passenger workings on the DN&S in the latter years, the exception of course being *City of Truro* which will be portrayed later. On 27 February 1960, though, a grime-encrusted 'Grange' class 4-6-0, No 6833 *Calcot Grange*, is at the head of a down goods about to enter the platform at Churn, heading towards Newbury and possibly destined for the Berks & Hants line and Westbury. No 6833 would outlive the DN&S line and was withdrawn from traffic in 1965 at the time of the wholesale slaughter of former GWR steam locomotives. *T. B. Owen/Colour-Rail T26*

*Right:* Springtime at Compton sees the first of S. C. Townroe's views of the DN&S line taken following the start of regular Eastleigh workings through to Didcot. At this time Stephen Townroe was the Motive Power Superintendent at Eastleigh and as such the line came under his jurisdiction as far as Enborne Junction. Aside from being a professional railwayman, he was also an enthusiast — preferably for Southern stock, it must be said — and he was shrewd enough to capture on film much of what would soon be consigned to memory. In this 1953 photograph, a northbound Didcot '22xx' is shown about to leave past the signalbox and goods yard, with the whole scene still in the colour scheme of its pre-nationalisation owners. *S. C. Townroe/Colour-Rail*

*Right:* South of Compton was one of two level crossings on the line and then came the stopping place at Hampstead Norris, seen here in the early 1960s. Here the station building was unique in that the DN&S style of cottage had not been provided, although the accommodation was extended over the years, with the top of the original signalbox being resited on to the platform and used as a parcels store. With the doubling that took place in 1942/3, a new brick signalbox was provided to the then standard ARP design, which was located on the opposite side of the line.
*Kevin Robertson collection*

*Left:* Between Hampstead Norris and Hermitage a new stopping place had been opened by the GWR in 1933 in an attempt to attract more local traffic. Named 'Pinewood Halt', it served the north end of the Hermitage area at a time when residential development was spreading close to the railway. It was originally provided with a single platform, but a second platform face was built following the doubling.
*Chris Webb*

*Right:* The second level crossing on the line was at Fishers Lane, between Hermitage and Newbury. Regrettably, not a single colour view of Hermitage has been located. Both the level crossings on the line were hand operated, with the crossing keeper 'Always in attendance' — at least, according to the Sectional Appendix. Passing Fishers Lane, heading south, is the unusual combination of 'WD' 2-8-0 No 90565 and pannier tank No 8720 at the head of what may well be an engineer's train, c1960.
*Kevin Robertson collection*

*Above:* Colour views of the diesel service that operated briefly between Didcot and Newbury in the 1961/2 period are rare, although here the single car has been captured crossing over the River Lambourn bridge near Shaw, north of Newbury. For the benefit of passengers, these vehicles were provided with a roller-type destination blind in the centre front window which included Lambourn in the list of names. This was somewhat superfluous as the Lambourn service from Newbury had been withdrawn at the start of 1960 and was never operated by this type of unit. *Chris Webb*

*Right:* With the exception of Shawford Junction (shown later in the book), colour views of the actual junctions of the DN&S are conspicuous by their absence. The nearest example is this stunning portrait of one of the 'Warship' class diesels in full flight westwards at Newbury East Junction, showing the trackwork of the DN&S joining the main line from the left. The signalbox of the same name stands by the line and was equipped with a frame of 84 levers. It remained in use until the spread of MAS (multiple-aspect signalling) from Reading. *Chris Webb*

*Above left:* A short distance on from Newbury East Junction was Newbury station itself. Originally a flyover had been proposed here but this was never built and instead DN&S trains would use the Berks & Hants main line for a distance of just under two miles before turning south again at Enborne Junction. On this occasion, on 23 July 1958, No 7708 enters Newbury under what was then the A34 bypass at Newbury. *Kevin Robertson collection*

*Left:* Watched by an admiring audience, No 5923 *Colston Hall* runs through Newbury on the up through line at the head of the 9.35am Paignton–Paddington West Country 'runner'. Trains for Didcot would use either the up platform line or the bay just behind the engine, whilst those for Southampton would similarly use the down platform or the bay, dependent upon the timetable. *G. H. Hunt/ Colour-Rail/BRW 1359*

*Above:* 'T9' No 30313 is seen again, this time blowing off noisily as it waits to head north from Newbury on 28 April 1959. Of the three bay platforms that once existed at Newbury, this is the only one still in use, although regrettably no longer for Didcot. Likewise, beyond the bridge is the capacious goods yard which is also now but a memory. *Alan Jarvis*

*Left:* Aside from being used for Didcot-bound trains, the up bay line at Newbury was also used for stopping services to Reading. Indeed, it remains in use for the same purpose today. On this occasion one of the former GWR streamlined railcars, now numbered W12W, waits against the buffer stops, almost ready for the return working. *Colour-Rail/DE943*

*Above:* During the 1950s a number of passenger workings were given over to new BR Class 4 haulage, with the same type also appearing on freight workings. Here, on 5 June 1954, 15-month-old No 76010 disgorges its passengers at Newbury's down platform before continuing the journey south to Enborne Junction and Winchester. Rebuilt in 1909/10 by the GWR, partly at the expense of the then independent DN&S company, Newbury station is basically unaltered today. A threat to demolish the main buildings and footbridge has fortunately now receded and it still boasts up and down through lines as well as platform faces for the relief lines in either direction. *Kevin Robertson collection*

South from Newbury the double line continued to the first station at Woodhay, after which the route was only ever single track with passing loops at intervals. Woodhay station would have been more appropriately named Highclere, as it was geographically closer to the village of that name than the next station, which actually bore the name of Highclere. If this appears confusing to the reader, spare a thought for the unfortunate passenger who could find himself or herself stranded at the wrong station, with no alternative but a long wait or a walk of some miles along country roads. Woodhay at one time allegedly also had one platform in Hampshire and the other in Berkshire, although a change in county boundaries did at least resolve *that* issue. Today, the site of the station has completely disappeared under the Newbury bypass and no more is it possible to witness a scene such as a 2-6-0 Mogul awaiting departure north, with what appears to be an enthusiastic photographer racing ahead, as seen in this February 1960 photograph. *Gerald Daniels*

The next stopping place on from Woodhay was at Highclere, so named as it was the nearest stop to the ancestral home of Lord Carnarvon at Highclere Castle who had fought vigorously for the railway to be built in the late 19th century. Here again was the standard DN&S-style station building fronting a passing loop, with a small goods yard beyond. Most of the original stations were to a similar design, the station building also affording private accommodation for the incumbent stationmaster and his family. The loop was extended twice at the station during its lifetime but was taken out of use in 1955 for operating economy. Shortly after this it was severed at each end, although, as can be seen, the now redundant former up platform line has been freshly reballasted. Likewise, the station was repainted just prior to closure. Incurring such costs against limited revenue meant that a deficit was inevitable, although such massaging of the figures to speed closure was hardly necessary as in the last years the number of passengers south of Newbury rarely exceeded single figures in a day. *Gerald Daniels*

*Left:* Class 4 No 76062 is seen entering the down platform at Burghclere station from the north with an Eastleigh goods on Saturday 5 March 1960. Here the service will cross an up passenger working. Burghclere had received an extended loop as part of the 1942/3 wartime improvements programme, which, according to the crews, considerably improved track quality where new lines had been laid. Burghclere had also originally boasted a private siding serving a lime quarry but this officially ceased in 1946, having been out of use for some time prior to that date.
*T. B. Owen/Colour-Rail/T215*

*Above:* A few minutes later and the up passenger service referred to in the previous caption is now at the platform with No 6302 at its head. On this occasion there was more than the usual handful of passengers visible as these photographs were taken on the last day of regular passenger workings. As with Woodhay and Highclere, this station was also inappropriately named, the village of Burghclere being some two miles to the north, hard by what was named Highclere station. Protestations by the DN&S company in the early years of the line were to no avail and its attempts to have this stopping place renamed Sydmonton were refused by the GWR. Ironically, today it is still possible to find a road sign nearby pointing to 'Burghclere Stn'.
*T. B. Owen/Colour-Rail/T216*

GREAT WESTERN RAILWAY
—
NOTICE
All Persons are warned not to
trespass upon the Railways or Stations
of the Company. and Notice is hereby
given that, pursuant to the provisions
of the Company's Acts. every person who
trespasses upon any such railway or
station in such manner as to expose
himself to danger or risk of danger
renders himself liable to a penalty of
Forty shillings. and in default of
payment. to one month's imprisonment
for every such offence.
By order.

*Above:* Not to be confused with the similar sounding location in the Midlands, we next come to Litchfield (Hants) — or ''Aunts', as the porter used to call out. This was another of the intermediate stopping places that succumbed to economy in 1955 with the removal of the passing loop, leaving just a single platform face and a small yard. Little traffic ever originated from this station and the *Hampshire Chronicle* newspaper recorded, probably very accurately, just before the line closed that the porter in charge here would have to be a man well used to his own company and capable of making his own amusements. *Gerald Daniels*

*Left:* Despite starting as an independent company, the little DN&S was all but in name a Great Western line from the outset, as standard GWR notices and equipment predominated. One example which lasted to the end was this delightful enamel sign at Litchfield warning of the dire consequences of trespass — 40s of proper money or £2 to those brought up in a metric age. *Gerald Daniels*

Between Litchfield and Whitchurch the railway ran parallel to the A34, although for some distance it was hidden from it by trees and cuttings. In places the formation, so well cared for by the gangers, clearly showed evidence of the double track width provided from the outset even though a single track was all that had ever been laid.

This is another of Stephen Townroe's views, his professional capacity meaning he had unrestricted access to the footplate, no doubt to the envy of many.
*S. C. Townroe/Colour-Rail*

*Left:* Steaming north towards Litchfield is a BR Class 4 '76xxx' on an Eastleigh-based Southampton to Didcot working. The grand plans of the DN&S promoters for a north-south trunk line taking traffic from the Midlands to the South Coast did not consider survival solely from the local community but that, in effect, is what the line did survive on for most of its life. Small wonder, then, that it was so well described by Mike Parsons as 'BR's rural crumb catcher'. *Gerald Daniels*

*Below left:* A cold February day in 1960 finds an unidentified '22xx' at the head of the ubiquitous three-coach rake plus van running south between Litchfield and Whitchurch. Had the original proposals been implemented there would have been a connection between the DN&S and LSWR West of England main line near to this point. However, although some earthworks were started, no track was ever laid. *Gerald Daniels*

*Right:* Midway between Newbury and Winchester was Whitchurch station, which was far more conveniently placed for the town compared to the former LSWR stopping place. The traffic generated outstripped all of the other DN&S stations, aside from at Winchester. This was also the only place on the southern section of the line where engines could take water en route. In this view looking north, it is just possible to see the bridge carrying the LSWR over the DN&S in the extreme distance. The standard DN&S building is on the down side, connected by a subway to the opposite platform with its small waiting shelter. The yard was behind the photographer and dealt with the usual coal and general merchandise as well as jam from a local manufacturer and quantities of watercress. *Gerald Daniels*

Seen from the approach side, most of the DN&S stations presented an appearance more like a country residence than a railway station. Indeed, since closure nearly all those that have survived have been sold and converted into spacious private houses. The building at Whitchurch was also given a single-storey extension at the south end, which was later rendered in keeping with the original building. Passengers were supposed to enter the station via the booking office, although in practice at all the stations excepting Winchester most would walk straight on to the platform before entering the booking office. *Rev D. Littlefair*

A clean black-liveried '22xx', No 2201, waits to depart south from Whitchurch in the last days of regular passenger working. In its final years the station was under the charge of Harry Hillier, a delightful man who did all he could to promote the line, although sadly to no avail. Harry was angry that no attempt was ever made to reduce costs by introducing diesel working south of Newbury, although in reality it is unlikely that this would have made much difference. Right to the end the station also presented a neat and tidy appearance and won several prizes in the annual station gardens competitions. Years earlier there had even been a goldfish pond on the platform, and the gardens had been tended by a one-legged porter. This man had lost his leg serving during World War 1 and returned to the railway after being discharged from the army. Despite his disability he would approach passengers on his crutches and offer to carry bags. The story has it that the passengers would then feel embarrassed and carry their own bags, but the man would still get a tip! *Colour-Rail/BRW 1229*

*Left:* The wartime improvements of 1942/3 have already been referred to and here is an example of one of the ARP-type signalboxes provided, of which nine were constructed on the DN&S. Functional and austere, eight survived until the end and were made slightly more comfortable over the years by respective signalman, with the aid of carpets, cushions and the like. Whitchurch signalbox stood on the side of the railway embankment and, although not apparent from the photograph, was supported on deep footings at the rear. It contained a frame of 27 levers and lasted in use until August 1964. Two years later, when this photograph was taken, it was still intact — Harry Hillier saw to it there was no vandalism. The author purchased from BR the complete contents for just £2 in the early 1970s. Regrettably, though, adulthood has meant that the items obtained at this time have long been scattered far and wide. *Rev D. Littlefair*

*Right:* With one exception, at Lodge Bridge, the wartime extensions of the loops allowed for a straight run in from either direction and a curved exit, the points at the far end of each loop being electrically operated by the signalman using a hand-generator. This was the view that would have been seen by the driver of a southbound train when entering Whitchurch, with the sand-drag and catch point on the right, responsible for the two spectacular freight derailments of 1954 and 1960 (both of which are depicted later in the book). Incidentally, after closure BR purloined one of the lower quadrant stop signals from Whitchurch for use temporarily near Micheldever on the Bournemouth main line. *Rev D. Littlefair*

*Above:* The distance from Whitchurch to the next station south at Sutton Scotney was approximately five miles. To break up the long section and thus afford greater line occupancy, an intermediate crossing place and signalbox were established in the 1940s at Lodge Bridge. This was an inhospitable location, high on an exposed embankment, and it is little wonder that it became known to the signalmen compelled to work it as 'Howls Lodge'. It lasted only from 1943 to 1950 and was demolished soon afterwards. Regrettably, no photographs appear to have survived from when it was in use, although Stephen Townroe has captured a Didcot '22xx' running along the site of the former crossing loop in the summer of 1953. *S. C. Townroe/Colour-Rail*

*Right:* Near Lodge Bridge there had been a short-lived wartime halt at Barton Stacey but this was gone by 1941. The location, though, was close to where No 2221 was photographed c1953 heading south along a formation clearly once suitable for a double track to have been laid. *S. C. Townroe/Colour-Rail*

*Left:* Sutton Scotney was originally the last station before Winchester, although this changed from 1909. In the last years of the line the railway here was known locally as the 'seven-penny' line, due to two signalmen, Jack Tanner and Ernie Penny! One of the pair was no doubt on duty as No 76017, the engine that went down the bank at Whitchurch in 1954, passes the signalbox bound for Eastleigh in February 1960. *Gerald Daniels*

*Above:* Sutton Scotney was the last of the standard-type DN&S stations with the basic crossing place and yard design. Increasing traffic over the years, particularly parcels, meant additional storage space was required, hence the hut nearest the photographer, on the left-hand platform. For some years a climbing rose adorned the goods shed with the initials 'GWR'. The men recounted that after 1950 it tended to wither and was never successfully altered to SR! *Gerald Daniels*

*Above:* Christmas Hill cutting south of Sutton Scotney sees a bank holiday excursion from Cleethorpes and Grimsby to Portsmouth and Southsea. The train, headed by another '43xx' Mogul, was captured travelling south shortly after midday — goodness knows what time it must have set out! Les Elsey, who took the photograph, recalled there appeared to have been some non-corridor stock towards the rear and the conditions for the unfortunate passengers who had endured such a journey are best left to the imagination! *Les Elsey*

*Right:* No 3210 is seen leaving Worthy Down for Winchester in August 1954. This stopping place had been provided in 1918 to serve what was then a new base for the Royal Flying Corps. By 1940 it was a naval air station and it still survives today as the base for the Royal Army Pay Corps. Traffic was always limited and was restricted to service personnel and stores. Even so, Worthy Down retained its island platform, loop and signalbox to the end, although the siding on the left was removed shortly after the photograph was taken. *Brian Swain/Colour-Rail/BRW1189*

South of Worthy Down a connection was provided with the main Southern route in 1942/3. This was used only sporadically and was equipped for up trains only. Intended as a relief for trains heading north, which could then avoid holding up other traffic at Shawford Junction, it would also have enabled the DN&S to remain a useful north-south link had the viaduct near Shawford been damaged by enemy action. Fortunately, it was never needed for this purpose. *Gerald Daniels*

In addition to the connection to Worthy Down from the Bournemouth main line at Winchester Junction, the Alton line diverged behind the signalbox (which remained in use until 1973) at Winchester Junction. The DN&S connection, however, had been curtailed some years earlier. With the facing connection taken out of use in 1950, it was then used solely for stock storage awaiting entry to Eastleigh Works. *Gerald Daniels*

*Left:* Another Eastleigh-based Standard design, this time No 75005, is seen heading north near Woodhams Farm, between King's Worthy and Worthy Down, on the last day of passenger service, 5 March 1960. *T. B. Owen/Colour-Rail/T29*

*Above:* Passing under the former LSWR main line near Winchester Junction in 1953 is 'T9' No 30285, bound for King's Worthy. The proximity of the two company's routes at this point had been the subject of discussion from very early on as to a possible connection, and several schemes were proposed over the years. One had even involved a relief to the main line around Winchester, whilst another, in the 1930s, was the total opposite and envisaged the abandonment of the DN&S so that part of its route could have been used for road improvements. Ironically, this is exactly what did happen some decades later. *S. C. Townroe/Colour-Rail*

*Left:* Heading south, King's Worthy was the last station before Winchester. The scene is sadly in the last years of the station, with the down loop and platform removed following the 1955 attempt at economies. Today there is not the slightest vestige of a railway ever having existed here and the trackbed forms part of the A34 trunk road. *Gerald Daniels*

*Right:* Winchester at last, and here the DN&S station showed more allegiance to Paddington than to its independent roots. The main station building was a typical late 19th century design, also used at Ross-on-Wye. (Almost a century later Kidderminster on the Severn Valley Railway would be re-created to similar type.) The station itself was not particularly far from the centre of Winchester but was little known for much of its life and this was reflected in the limited passenger revenue. Even so it did at one time boast facilities for first, second and third class passengers, as well as a foot-warmer store for those who could afford such luxuries. *Rev D. Littlefair*

*Right:* Winchester was not always an easy location for photography, the 100ft-plus height of St Giles' Hill on the east side meaning the sun was in the right place for only a short time each day. St Giles' Hill had also to be cut back quite considerable when the line was being built, which led to a spectacular chalk fall a few years later. By the time this view was taken, though, trees and foliage had taken root on the hillside. In this view the camera is pointing south from the tunnel to the small timber waiting shelter on the down platform, with the footbridge and signalbox beyond. *Rev D. Littlefair*

*Above:* Entry for trains at Winchester from the north was through a 441yd tunnel at the north end of the station. The tunnel was on a slight curve and this measurement referred to the outside curve, which was of course slightly longer. As such, the ganger would receive tunnel allowance, something he would not get if it was less than ¼ mile (440yd)! Winchester was also where GWR locomotives would be changed to SR engines, a practice which dated back to 1891 and which was abolished only in 1953. On this occasion, though, No 3206 will work through to Southampton and is seen in the down platform in April 1955.
*Brian Swain/Colour-Rail/BRW1188*

*Right:* For a period in 1957-8 *City of Truro* was the regular engine on the 12.42pm ex-Didcot and return 4.57pm working from Southampton. Not surprisingly, this superb machine attracted a not inconsiderable amount of interest and its appearance was well reported in the contemporary railway press. It is seen here standing at Winchester waiting to head north, the fireman seeming to prefer to fire in the station rather than when in the tunnel. *S. C. Townroe/Colour-Rail*

As a comparison with the photograph on the back cover of the book, this was the scene a few years later when dwindling passengers numbers meant little money was available for painting of either infrastructure, at this location, or trains. The track, though, does appear to have been recently ballasted. No 2226 pauses at an otherwise deserted station. *Kevin Robertson collection*

The 1950s, whilst witnessing a decline in passengers, did see an increase in freight using the route, much of this petrol and oil trains from Fawley to the Midlands. One of these is seen here with a brand-new Standard Class 4, No 76065, in charge of a heavy load of tanks. The fireman has a good head of steam ready for surmounting the various 1 in 106 banks northwards — he will need it all before reaching the summit of the climb, near Burghclere. *S. C. Townroe/Colour-Rail*

At nationalisation the whole route was initially taken under the control of the new Western Region, although the section south from Enborne was given over to the Southern Region in 1950. One of the outward changes that then took place was the renaming of Winchester as Winchester Chesil, to avoid confusion with the former Southern station of the same name. The plate proclaiming this change is seen in 1954 affixed to the running-in board on the platform. *Gerald Daniels*

The extreme winter of 1963 brought snow to Hampshire, the like of which has not been seen since. As far as the DN&S was concerned, the withdrawal of passenger services three years earlier meant that only freight would be disrupted, although the line was blocked in places for several days. Despite the weather, work would continue as normal — witness the signalman trudging back to his box with his water supply from the station one freezing afternoon at Winchester Chesil. *Doug Hannah*

*Left:* South of the passenger station a footpath linking nearby Chesil Street and St Giles Hill crossed the railway and provided another vantage point for the photographer. By the 1960s the signs of Southern ownership were present in that the signalbox had taken on the standard green and yellow paint scheme. The signalbox in this form dated from 1942, when it had been extended on the side nearest the photographer — the change in brick colour is just visible. At one time a power frame had been installed but this was replaced in 1932 by conventional working. The signals visible were, on the left, the down line to the yard, and, on the right, the down line to Shawford Junction starting. They had replaced a wooden bracket signal in 1948. *Doug Hannah*

*Right:* Beyond Winchester station the route curved gently, still keeping to the foot of the hill, before passing under East Hill Bridge. The railway was really single line here, to the left the track led to and from Shawford Junction whilst on the right was the down siding that led to the yard. In consequence of the running of the heavy oil trains, much of the route in the Winchester area was relaid with concrete sleepers, as seen here. It is said that after closure this track was recovered for use elsewhere. *Doug Hannah*

*Right:* The cramped facilities at Winchester passenger station meant that the goods yard and engine shed were located south of the station at Bar End. Facilities at the more commodious Bar End included a shed and turntable. Coaling, though, was undertaken by hand. Two engines were out-stationed here from Didcot although the design of the shed meant that as engine sizes increased it was possible for only part of each to be kept under cover. The shed was in use from 1885 until 1953, after which engine requirements were dealt with from Eastleigh. *S. C. Townroe/Colour-Rail*

*Left:* One of the reasons for the success of the DN&S at Winchester was its ability to handle goods better than at the cramped yard associated with the Southern station. For enthusiasts there was an ideal vantage point from a footbridge that spanned the yard neck, where generations of spotters would gather to watch the activity. In the early years almost every type of freight was handled, although as the years passed this slowly gave way to coal as the principal source of revenue. This 1960s view shows the yard still busy, although the former cattle pens on the right are no longer rail connected. The locomotive was No 80082. *Rev D. Littlefair*

*Below left:* South from Bar End the route turned southwest towards Shawford Junction. Had the DN&S been able to follow its intended route then the next station would have been at Twyford but that was never to be. Instead St Catherine's Hill provides a grandstand view of a '22xx' heading south. The Winchester bypass on the right is deserted. *S. C. Townroe/ Colour-Rail*

*Right:* This photograph was taken from the footplate of *City of Truro*, running south in the early afternoon only a mile or so before joining the former LSWR main line. The particular diagram worked by this engine was no doubt especially arranged by the WR so that its return from Southampton would see it collecting men from Eastleigh Locomotive Works before returning to Winchester with this particular engine at the head of the train. No harm in showing them what a proper engine could do . . ! *S. C. Townroe/Colour-Rail*

Just prior to joining the LSWR main line there was an overbridge followed by the viaduct at Hockley. This time a somewhat grimy '22xx' is at the head of Western Region stock that has come off the SR line and is running the two miles to Winchester as part of its journey north to Didcot. *S. C. Townroe/Colour-Rail*

The end of the DN&S proper sees No 3212 cautiously coming off the viaduct at Hockley heading towards Shawford Junction, where the single-line tablet will be given up. This section of line from Winchester to Shawford Junction was built only for a single track and was destined to be a bottleneck, particularly during the war years. *S. C. Townroe/Colour-Rail*

*Above:* Signalman Tom Timpson hands over the tablet to the fireman of a Winchester-bound passenger train. Aside from the first two miles to Winchester, all the other single-line sections on the DN&S were token worked, with the majority of exchanges being done using the set-down and pick-up posts. Despite the obvious deterioration that has taken place with the slide, it is well worthy of inclusion, as it shows the southern end of the DN&S route proper. *Kevin Robertson collection*

*Right:* After a life of just 75 years, a notice forewarned of the end to come. There would be no stay of execution as far as passenger traffic was concerned. *Gerald Daniels*

*Right:* Following the cessation of passenger workings, the complete route was available for freight, which showed a marked build-up in the early 1960s. One example is depicted here with an unidentified '76xxx' near Seven Barrows, south of Litchfield, on what may well be a fitted freight. Interestingly, alongside is the deserted A34. A generation later would see a total role reversal! *P. W. Goulder*

*Below right:* As the 1960s continued, 'D65xx' class locomotives — later known as the Class 33 or 'Cromptons' — began to appear on the various freight services. They were particularly used on the Bromford Bridge oil trains, which were also to be seen behind '9F' 2-10-0s, several of which type had been transferred to Eastleigh specially for this type of working. Here an unidentified Class 33 locomotive is heading north at Woodhay, passing what was reputed to be the tallest signal on the whole railway.

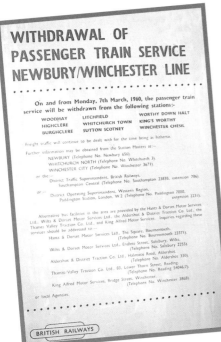

WITHDRAWAL OF
PASSENGER TRAIN SERVICE
NEWBURY/WINCHESTER LINE

On and from Monday, 7th March, 1960, the passenger train service will be withdrawn from the following stations:-

| | | |
|---|---|---|
| WOODHAY | LITCHFIELD | WORTHY DOWN HALT |
| HIGHCLERE | WHITCHURCH TOWN | KING'S WORTHY |
| BURGHCLERE | SUTTON SCOTNEY | WINCHESTER CHESIL |

Freight traffic will continue to be dealt with for the time being as hitherto.

Further information may be obtained from the Station Masters at:—
NEWBURY (Telephone No. Newbury 656).
WHITCHURCH NORTH (Telephone No. Whitchurch 3).
WINCHESTER CITY (Telephone No. Winchester 3671).

or the—
District Traffic Superintendent, British Railways,
Southampton Central (Telephone No. Southampton 23830, extension 786).

or—
District Operating Superintendent, Western Region,
Paddington Station, London, W 2 (Telephone No. Paddington 7000,
extension 2231).

Alternative bus facilities in the area are provided by the Hants & Dorset Motor Services Ltd., Wilts & Dorset Motor Services Ltd., the Aldershot & District Traction Co. Ltd., the Thames Valley Traction Co. Ltd., and King Alfred Motor Services. Inquiries regarding these services should be addressed to—
Hants & Dorset Motor Services Ltd., The Square, Bournemouth.
(Telephone No. Bournemouth 23371).
Wilts & Dorset Motor Services Ltd., Endless Street, Salisbury, Wilts.
(Telephone No. Salisbury 2255).
Aldershot & District Traction Co. Ltd., Halimote Road, Aldershot.
(Telephone No. Aldershot 330).
Thames Valley Traction Co. Ltd., 83, Lower Thorn Street, Reading.
(Telephone No. Reading 54046/7).
King Alfred Motor Services, Bridge Street, Winchester.
(Telephone No. Winchester 3868).

or local Agencies.

BRITISH RAILWAYS

*Above:* A special working is seen here, passing King's Worthy in 1962 with a BR Standard in charge of a mixed Southern rake. Following the removal of the loop at this station, the track remained slewed to its old formation and as such presented a 'dog-leg' to trains. This is clearly visible under the front of the train. In the background the yard still appears busy, with a Thames Trader lorry belonging to the coal merchant Bryer Ash in its bright red livery. *Les Elsey*

*Right:* Rail tours were another feature of the last years. The 'Hampshire Hog' of 18 April 1964, traversing ground away from its home county, is here paused at Hampstead Norris on a miserable wet day. The engine in charge is an Ivatt 2-6-2T. *Roy Hobbs*

*Left:* One of the most famous tours of the south of England in the early 1960s was the 'East Midlander' organised by the RCTS. For the DN&S section of the tour an unrebuilt 'West Country' Pacific, No 34038 *Lynton*, was provided and it is seen here on 9 May 1964 running south between Burghclere and Litchfield, on the way to its next port of call at Eastleigh Works. *Roy Hobbs*

*Above:* A few years earlier another tour to run on DN&S metals was the 'Solent Limited' on 30 April 1961. This commenced at Waterloo and ran first to Portsmouth and then Fareham, including both Gosport and the former Meon Valley lines in its itinerary. From there it went to Southampton and Eastleigh Works and then travelled via the DN&S to Newbury before returning to Waterloo via Reading and Ascot. You needed to be truly dedicated for such a day! However, many obviously were, as can be seen from the number gathered around the front of 'T9' No 30117, paused for a photographic stop at Highclere. *Kevin Robertson collection*

*Above:* A feature for which the final years of the DN&S are also remembered are the three spectacular derailments that occurred within a nine-year span. The first was at Whitchurch on 23 September 1954 when No 76017 was unable to stop at the starting signal and ended up running through the sand-drag, before coming to rest against some mature trees on the embankment. Fortunately, there were no serious casualties. The cause of the accident was attributed to the lack of brake power available to the crew. *Brian Swain/Colour-Rail/BS4*

*Right:* An initial assessment by Stephen Townroe confirmed that two cranes would be needed to right the engine but in the interim cables were attached to prevent any further movement. The resultant debris that had piled up behind the engine was also cleared, allowing normal services to resume. *S. C. Townroe/Colour-Rail*

*Above:* Recovery eventually took place on Sunday, 3 October, using the steam cranes from both Fratton and Eastleigh. The engine was righted and after inspection towed back to Eastleigh for repair. No 76017 is now preserved on the Mid-Hants Railway and it is said that the scars of 1954 are still visible — if you know where to look. *S. C. Townroe/Colour-Rail*

*Right:* An almost identical incident occurred some six years later, on 12 February 1960, when sister engine No 76026 embedded itself in the same piece of soft ground. Once again, lack of brake power was the attributed cause. Fortunately, the bed of sleepers laid years earlier was still intact and so No 76026 only fell part of the way down the embankment before the sleepers and some trees arrested its progress. As an added safety feature, however, the dome cover was removed and a wire hawser attached between the locomotive and some mature trees on the opposite side of the railway. In this way further movement of the locomotive was prevented until recovery could take place. *S. C. Townroe/Colour-Rail*

*Left:* Recovery again involved two steam cranes; this time the Eastleigh and Salisbury crews were involved, again under the direction of Stephen Townroe. *S. C. Townroe/Colour-Rail*

*Above:* A close-up of the Eastleigh crane at work. Close co-operation was essential between the drivers of the cranes, who had to have instructions relayed to them from the ground by a banksman. *S. C. Townroe/Colour-Rail*

*Above:* Seen from the cricket ground on the east side of the line, No 76026 hangs precariously as it is guided back to the rails. In normal times there was a challenge to the local cricket teams here as to who could score a six by hitting the ball over the trees and across the railway. *Brian Swain/Colour-Rail BS2*

*Right:* The locomotive is back on the rails again and ready for inspection, prior to setting off for Eastleigh. Fortunately, the chalky subsoil which constituted much of the embankment meant that damage on both occasions was relatively superficial. *Brian Swain/Colour-Rail BS19*

*Left:* Back at Shawford Junction the recalcitrant engine is formed at the rear of the convoy, en route for Eastleigh. The train is signalled on to the down relief line at this point, which would take the procession around the back of Shawford station.
*S. C. Townroe/Colour-Rail*

*Below left:* A final view of the Whitchurch incident, with the Salisbury crane also at Shawford Junction, before travelling home via Eastleigh. Aside from accidents and derailments, which were hopefully not too common an occurrence, the cranes would be used within their respective areas for civil engineering purposes such as bridge replacements. Additionally, the Eastleigh crane was often used around the works yard for lifting boilers and other heavy items.
*S. C. Townroe/Colour-Rail*

*Right:* The final accident of the trilogy was the most devastating. It occurred at Hockleys Hole, between Highclere and Burghclere, on Saturday morning, 23 March 1963. On that occasion a diesel-hauled freight jumped the rails in the cutting, the resultant snatch causing a monumental pile-up of wagons that almost filled the cutting. Fortunately again, there were no serious injuries, although the Eastleigh Guard, Bernie Briggs, was understandably bruised, having been thrown around in his van.
*S. C. Townroe/Colour-Rail*

*Left:* The cause of the accident had its origins back at Didcot, where an earlier down freight was cancelled as it was considered to have insufficient vehicles. The vehicles were added, instead, to the next down working. The result was that a light match truck in the centre of the train did not posses enough weight to keep it stable. Entering the cutting, a form of oscillation was set up and eventually the wheels of this vehicle left the track, damaging sleepers and rails until the following vehicles were forced to leave the rails. *S. C. Townroe/Colour-Rail*

*Above:* Recovery was made more difficult on the single-track line as the site could be approached by rail only from each end so, with the Eastleigh crane working from the south and the Old Oak Common crane arriving via Newbury, salvage operations began. Additionally, the permanent way staff were required to re-lay sleepers and track for both the cranes to run on and to aid the recovery of vehicles. *S. C. Townroe/Colour-Rail*

Watched by an inquisitive group, the Eastleigh crane is forced to lift a tank car high off the ground in order to gain sufficient clearance. In the background, obscured by the steam from the crane, were several fire appliances, their presence being required because of the empty tank cars. Due to the dangers of possible flammable vapour from the empty tanks, there was a ban on naked lights which extended to the gas ring normally used by the men in the crane's mess van for a 'brew'. The fact the crane was coal fired was accepted, though! *Brian Swain/Colour-Rail BS A23*

Once the vehicles were back on the rails, they were pulled back to Burghclere by 'D65xx' class No D6549 for examination, the diesel being used because of the fire risk. At the north end the wagons that had been salvaged had to go as far as Woodhay, as the loop at Highclere was no longer in use.
*Brian Swain/Colour-Rail BS A29*

A final view of the scene sees operations drawing to a close. Recovery took several days and many wondered if the line would reopen. It did, however, and remained open for through traffic until 9 August 1964. At the far end of the accident scene the Old Oak Common crane has been brought by a WR 4-6-0 — no ban on steam here!

Several different steam engines were used for this task over the clear-up days including No 7817 *Carrington Manor* and on one occasion an unidentified 'Castle' — a type normally banned from the DN&S route. *S. C. Townroe/Colour-Rail*

*Right:* The final months of the DN&S saw periods of inactivity interspersed with flurries of trains, many of these being 'box-to-box' specials rather than regular timetabled goods. Accordingly, at times there would be little for the signalmen to do, although all the boxes were required to remain open 24 hours daily. *Doug Hannah*

*Below right:* A last glimpse at the type of freight traffic that the DN&S was ideal at dealing with shows a '9F' 2-10-0 coming off the branch at Shawford Junction, on to the 1943 relief line bound for Eastleigh and then Fawley. This type of traffic would later be lost to new pipelines, although in recent years there has been a remarkable increase in freight container movement from Southampton Docks. The DN&S could have handled such goods admirably, but unfortunately it would not survive to see it. *Steam & Sail*

*Left:* From 1964 to 1966, when the last section of the route at Winchester Chesil was closed, a number of local specials were run. One of these is seen here with a former 'B4' dock tank, No 30096, on Hockley Viaduct, en route from Chesil to Southampton. *Roy Hobbs*

*Right:* The final days see the yard at Bar End now a shadow of its former busy days. This time an LCGB working has left Chesil, passing an almost deserted yard behind an Ivatt 2-6-2T in May 1965. *Maurice Graves*

*Below right:* The end is nigh! The dreams of the promoters and shareholders are unfulfilled. A line where men spent their working lives is abandoned, unwanted by a regime where duplicate routes and consideration for possible future traffic needs are irrelevant. In this final view the demolition contractors have moved in at Winchester. Soon the site will be totally razed, to be replaced by a car park, and *City of Truro* will no longer call on its way to and from Southampton. *Kevin Robertson collection*